Build That Team!

Readymade Tools for Team Improvement

Edited by
Steve Smith

KOGAN
PAGE

QUEST QUALITY

YOURS TO HAVE AND TO HOLD
BUT NOT TO COPY

First published in 1997

Kogan Page Limited
120 Pentonville Road
London N1 9JN

© Quest Worldwide Education Ltd

British Library Cataloguing in Publication Data

A CIP record for this book is available from the British Library.

ISBN 0 7494 2483 4

Typeset by Florencetype Ltd, Stoodleigh, Devon
Printed in England by Clays Ltd, St Ives plc

Contents

Introduction

Why use teams?

Organisations are composed of individuals, yet there is increasing emphasis on forming teams and helping them to work effectively. There are many reasons for this:

- Teams bring together skills and experiences that collectively exceed those of any individual. Consequently, teams can respond to a variety of challenges, eg process improvement, product development or customer service, more readily and more effectively.

- Teams encourage cross-functional working which can significantly improve processes and overall performance.

- Teams can be more creative than individuals by challenging others' assumptions and encouraging a 'fresh pair of eyes'.

- Working in teams, people are better able to handle change. Therefore change can take place more effectively and with greater commitment.

- Teams are often more fun than working in isolation and this can improve performance.

How to use this Toolbox

For many of us, the ability to work successfully in teams is not a naturally acquired skill – it needs guidance and support. A toolbox is a very efficient (and effective!) way of providing practical hints and tips.

This toolbox is designed for team leaders, facilitators, team members or managers working with teams on improvement projects of any kind.

It contains a number of essential tools for:

- getting started on project work
- team building and working together
- evaluating and reviewing team performance
- disbanding teams.

For each tool there is a description of:

- what it is
- how to use it
- how it helps.

How to use it

- Decide what stage your team is at and the sort of help it needs.

- Refer to the index to identify the tools available to help you at this stage.

- Select the tool most appropriate to your specific need.

- Follow the 'How it's done' instructions.

- Review the success of the tool and how you could use it again in the future.

How it helps

This toolbox:

- offers the team leader (or others) a number of **easy to use, tried and tested techniques** for solving team problems and building team effectiveness

- increases the likelihood of **full participation and involvement** of everyone in a team

- will lead to **better** and **quicker** results through **effective teamwork.**

Tools index

Alphabetical tools index

1 Teams: an overview

What Makes an Effective Team

What it is

It is difficult to build an effective team without understanding the characteristics of effective teams.

This checklist can be used to plan the development of a new team or to review the progress of an existing one in order to improve performance.

How to use it

1. Review the checklist.

2. Identify those elements which you need to focus on most to set up/improve your team.

3. Develop an action plan to tackle the elements you have identified.

HINT! *EFFECTIVE TEAMS ARE GREATER THAN THE SUM OF THEIR PARTS*

Effective teams:

✔ Have clear **goals** and **objectives**

✔ **Share responsibility** for those goals among team members

✔ **Measure their progress towards the goals**

✔ Are fairly **small** (less than 10 people)

✔ Have the necessary **blend of skills** (technical, problem solving, and interpersonal)

✔ Have the **resources** needed to do the job

✔ Have agreed **groundrules** for working together

✔ Have allocated appropriate **role(s)** to each member

✔ Have developed and agreed **working practices** and processes to get things done

✔ **Support** each other by listening, responding constructively and helpfully

✔ **Recognise** individual and team success

✔ **Handle conflict** constructively and openly

✔ Produce a **collective** output which achieves the goals as effectively, efficiently and creatively as possible

✔ **Share leadership** as appropriate within the team (it is not just for the formal leader).

How it helps

An effective team is more than a group of individuals. Teamwork does not 'just happen' it needs to be worked on. This tool outlines the characteristics of effective teams. It can be used for planning, review and improvement.

Once you have identified the particular aspect of teamworking that you need to address, use this toolbox to find out how to go about it.

Pre-empting Team Failure

What it is

It is important to understand why teams fail and what you can do to avoid this. This tool outlines the typical reasons why teams go wrong and the early symptoms you may see. Use it to both avoid and tackle potential pitfalls.

How to use it

- Review the checklist on reasons why teams fail.

- If your team is already experiencing difficulties, identify the particular reasons why. If you are being proactive before problems arise, identify the most likely stumbling blocks you may encounter.

- Develop an action plan to address these issues before they grow into major problems.

Teams fail because of:

✗ Unclear goals and objectives

✗ Non-measurable goals

✗ Ill-defined boundaries and responsibilities

✗ Inappropriate members, so key skills/knowledge that are needed are missing

✗ Lack of training in teamworking and problem-solving for members

✗ Inappropriate leadership style and behaviours

✗ Ineffective meetings

✗ Unwillingness of the team to accept responsibility

✗ Individually oriented reward and/or recognition

✗ Functional resistance and politics (to a cross-funtional team)

✗ Inappropriate use of a team, given time constraints, etc or as a substitute for an unpopular policy/ decision

✗ Stifling of individualism or individual creativity

✗ Failure to disband a team once it has served its purpose.

The early symptoms of these problems can include:

- **no shows** – team members are consistently absent.

- **arrive late/leave early** – team members consistently arrive after the meeting begins or leave before important business is completed.

- **substitutes** – team members begin to send other people in their place. This is especially troublesome when the substitutes are neither briefed nor empowered to make decisions.

- **chronic complaining** – team members complain after the team has been in existence for some time. The team climate should be relaxed and informal.

- **domination** – a few team members monopolise the discussions and unduly influence team decisions.

- **drop outs** – members seem disinterested. They may show up but they are not involved.

- **missed deadlines** – be concerned when members consistently miss deadlines for producing work and nobody's upset!

- **distant discussion** – members regularly talk about items not on the agenda and not related to the work of the team. Time seems to be wasted and no one seems to be bothered by it.

- **lack of focus** – team members either cannot state the mission or goal of the team, or there are very different views of the mission or goal among the members.

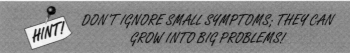

HINT! DON'T IGNORE SMALL SYMPTOMS, THEY CAN GROW INTO BIG PROBLEMS!

How it helps

Awareness of the reasons for team failure can be very helpful when setting up a new team as the pitfalls can largely be avoided by careful planning and team building.

If, however, you are already experiencing the symptoms use this tool to identify the likely causes.

The Life Cycle of a Project Team

What it is

Every project team goes through a series of steps to achieve results. This process map describes the main steps.

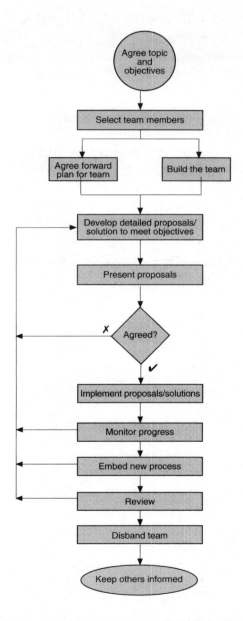

How to use it

Use the process map to plan overall what needs to be done in your team. The other tools in this and the other Quest Toolboxes can then be used as appropriate at each step.

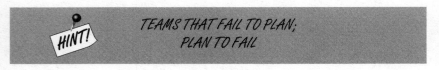

HINT! *TEAMS THAT FAIL TO PLAN, PLAN TO FAIL*

How it helps

Without adequate planning a project team is likely to fail. This tool outlines the main steps which should be part of the plan and suggests which tools are likely to be useful at each step.

2 Get started

Select an Improvement Project

What it is

As a team leader you may be asked by the executive team, a director or other manager to form a team to work on a specific project. You may however be confronted by a large number of potential projects, all apparently worthwhile, from which you must choose. This tool will give you some ideas on how to select the right project.

How to use it

1. Review the following checklist of the most common errors in project selection:

> ✗ Selecting a process that no-one is really interested in – the work will collapse at the first hurdle
>
> ✗ Selecting a solution instead of a process – don't jump to conclusions before you start, you might be wrong
>
> ✗ Selecting something that's already being improved by others or is in transition
>
> ✗ Choosing something too big or with unclear boundaries so that the project gets out of control
>
> ✗ Not clarifying specific objectives which the project must achieve
>
> ✗ Not focusing on projects which will clearly contribute to the overall goal(s) of the organisation
>
> ✗ Choosing something which can't be measured so you don't know how you're doing.

2. Are you guilty of any of these? Does it explain why you are making slow or no progress?

3. Can you make it work or would it be better to abandon your project and select something more valuable?

4. If you have not yet selected your project, review the following checklist to help you choose:

Choose a project that:

✓ Will have a clear ultimate benefit to external customers

✓ Requires little help from outside the team

✓ Looks at a process with a relatively short cycle time, so you can measure the effect quickly

✓ Is not already being reviewed or changed by someone else

✓ Is relatively simple, with clear start and end points

✓ Is important to both team members and customers

✓ Is something a substantial number of managers agree is important – you'll achieve their cooperation more readily

✓ Will give highly visible and measurable results (particularly for your first project).

---

5. Once you have chosen your topic or agreed to accept a topic which has been given to you, you must go on to clarify your goals and objectives and select your team members.

How it helps

Topic selection is the first step in undertaking a project which will be of real value for your business. This tool will help you make the right decision.

BEWARE OF 'USING A SLEDGEHAMMER TO CRACK A NUT'. ONLY SET UP A TEAM IF IT'S ABSOLUTELY NECESSARY

Establish Goals and Objectives

What it is

Goals give a team something to aim at which can be quite broad and can be achieved in a variety of ways. An example: 'To improve productivity substantially'. They are short, general statements of purpose and direction.

Objectives are very clear statements of what output you need to achieve. 'To reduce paper waste by 50% by year end.'

Effective objectives are more comprehensive and should be **SMART**:

Specific: Express objectives in terms of the specific results you want to achieve not in terms of the activities needed to achieve them, ie outputs not inputs. Avoid ambiguity.

Measurable: Identify what measures you will use to judge success. Make them as quantifiable and specific as possible, eg time/quantity/quality/cost. Use customer-related as well as internal measures.

Agreed: Team should have the opportunity to discuss and buy-in to the objective rather than simply have it imposed.

Realistic: Neither too easy so that talents are under-used, nor too difficult so that the team may burn out. Take past performance into account in assessing realism. Be sure the objective is achievable given the resource available and the demands of other priorities.

Timebound: Include a date by which the objective should be achieved and also interim milestones and review points if the overall timescale is long. Choose an appropriate timeframe relative to the complexity of the task.

It is also helpful to identify the relative priority between objectives, if there is more than one.

As a team you may be given a goal and left to set the objective(s) or simply given an overall corporate goal and left to set goals and objectives for your team. There may also be objectives for each individual within the team. This tool outlines the characteristics of effective objectives and how to go about agreeing them.

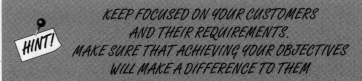

KEEP FOCUSED ON YOUR CUSTOMERS AND THEIR REQUIREMENTS. MAKE SURE THAT ACHIEVING YOUR OBJECTIVES WILL MAKE A DIFFERENCE TO THEM

How to use it

1. It is not enough to understand the characteristics of effective objectives. It is also important to use a process to set them which involves and empowers those whose job it is to achieve the objectives. The following process map outlines a way of achieving this:

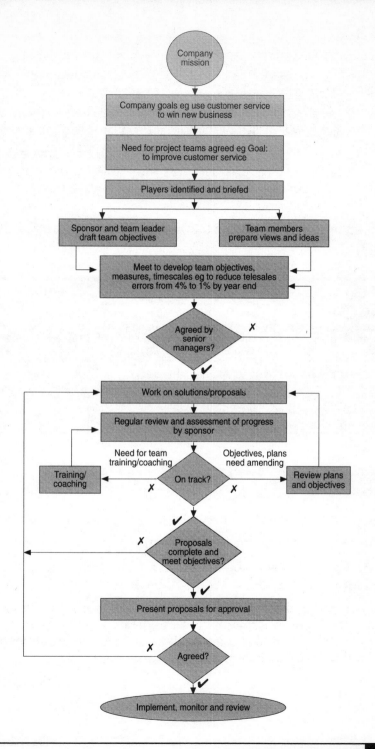

2. Review the process map. Which steps have you done/not done? How effective were they? What specifically do you need to do to ensure that your team has clear goals and SMART objectives?

3. The level to which team members are involved in the decisions within the objective setting process may vary.

Clearly, the more committed they are to the objectives, the more likely they are to put effort into making it happen – commitment can be the result of greater involvement in the decision making process.

As a team leader you have a choice of styles you can use at this stage:

Tell	Consult	Joint	Delegate
No commitment comes from the decision making process. Any commitment comes because the team members feel it is a good decision anyway.	Some commitment comes because their views may have influenced your decision.	Significant commitment comes from involvement in the decision making process.	Much commitment comes because they themselves have made the decisions.

You must choose the appropriate style to use given:

- the knowledge and experience of the team
- the degree of freedom available in setting the objective
- the time available to reach a decision.

4. As you progress, seek feedback from the team to check their reactions to the style you have adopted.

If you are unable to involve team members in developing and setting the team objectives it is important to involve them in planning how to achieve them as this can be equally successful in winning their commitment. How can you do this?

How it helps

Establishing goals and objectives takes time, effort and skill. The benefits of doing it, however, far outweigh the difficulties.

Establishing goals and objectives will help you to:

- ensure the team's work is relevant and adds value
- have more control over resources and actions
- know what people are working on
- coordinate individual efforts
- have an overall picture of progress
- assess performance (team and individual)
- identify problems early
- look ahead and anticipate change
- improve communication in your team.

It also helps the team member because each will have:

- clearer direction, realistic expectations and defined boundaries
- more freedom to get on with the job
- the means for receiving feedback
- a way of identifying training and development needs.

GOALS GIVE A SENSE OF PURPOSE AND DIRECTION, SPECIFIC OBJECTIVES GIVE PERFORMANCE MEASURES

Clarify Roles and Select Team Members

What it is

A very important step in establishing an effective project team is to select the right people.

Project roles

There are four key roles involved:

1. **Sponsor** – who actively supports the team from 'outside', secures resources, clears the pathway and ensures the team is 'hooked' into the organisation – effectively the 'internal customer' for the team.

2. **Team leader** – who leads the improvement team.

3. **Facilitator** (sometimes referred to as a coach or advisor) – who can provide practical guidance and support to the sponsor, leader and team members on how to operate effectively.

4. **Team members** – who carry out projects and implement improvements.

(For larger projects, there may also be a commissioner. This role is not included here for simplicity – refer to Quest's 'Make things happen!' Toolbox, if you feel it is appropriate to your project.)

How to use it

1. Review the descriptions of the roles and the individuals available.

This tool outlines the key roles which must be filled and the characteristics of the individuals who should fill them.

Sponsor

The sponsor ensures that the improvement team has the support of senior line management. The role of the sponsor is to:

- Provide a link to senior line management and company wide activity
- Secure the necessary resources for the team
- Support, show active interest but not lead the project
- Approve (but not dictate) the contract for the team
- Provide approval for implementing solutions.

Team leader

The role of the team leader is to:

- Manage the improvement team and its activities
- Liaise with the team sponsor to agree plans and discuss issues
- Enrol appropriate partners (customers, suppliers, technical experts)
- Allocate resources to the project (with sponsor)
- Break down functional barriers; resolve functional conflicts
- Empower project team members to identify and implement improvements
- Drive and stimulate improvements
- Provide reports to management on progress.

Team members

Team members will be involved in improvement teams because:

- they are part of the process which is being improved, or
- they are customers/suppliers of the process, or
- they want to be involved and are enthusiastic.

They should therefore have a stake in the outcome.

Team members need to:

- See team membership as part of their job and not as an intrusion or addition

- Contribute during meetings
    - sharing knowledge and experience
    - using skills
    - listening and asking questions
    - helping others to participate
    - if appropriate, take turns to chair the meeting.

- Carry out tasks between meetings, such as:
    - data gathering
    - testing solutions
    - measuring improvements.

- Take joint ownership and therefore share responsibility for the effectiveness of the team.

 BEWARE OF ALWAYS CHOOSING THE MOST 'POPULAR' PEOPLE – OTHERS MAY BE EQUALLY SUITABLE

Facilitator

The role of the facilitator in supporting an improvement team is to:

- Be an enthusiastic supporter of the team

- Provide guidance and support to the leader, sponsor and if appropriate, team members on specific issues

- Facilitate the process by helping with planning meetings, interpersonal issues etc.

- Train or coach in specific tools or techniques

- Identify and help address blockages.

2. Decide on the key roles: sponsor and leader.

3. Decide (given the experience and skills of the sponsor and leader) if a facilitator or coach is required and if so who to approach.

4. Identify the range of skills and knowledge needed by team members.

5. Develop a list of the minimum number of individuals required to provide these skills and knowledge (beware of making the team too large).

6. Gain agreement from all the individuals concerned and/or their manager to take part and agree the task for the first meeting.

How it helps

Understanding of the roles to be filled and choosing the right people to fill these roles are two vital aspects of establishing an effective, high performing team. This tool outlines what is required and how to go about it.

Set Groundrules

What it is

When a group of individuals come together to work as a team on a specific project they may find it helpful to establish a set of 'groundrules' to ensure they work effectively together. This can apply as much to a group who have worked together before as to one that hasn't.

How to use it

1. At the first meeting divide the group into pairs and ask the pairs to list any groundrules they feel are vital to the efficient working of the group.

2. If the group is small, you can simply discuss the issue all together – not in pairs.

3. Give them 5 minutes then ask the group or pairs to volunteer their points to you. Make a master list on a flipchart, as below:

Possible groundrules

- Be open and honest

- Listen to everyone's views

- Respect each other's experience

- Finish meetings on time

- Everyone must participate

- The role of Note-taker rotates each meeting

- Hand your mobile phones in at the door

(Further examples of groundrules can be found in the tool 'Run Effective Meetings'.)

---

4. Briefly review the list with the group, emphasising any rules you know to be particularly relevant, eg timekeeping.

5. Try to gain everyone's agreement to the rules then use them at your periodic team reviews to check that everyone is abiding by them and they are helpful.

How it helps

Groundrules are a very effective way of gaining agreement on how a team is going to work together. They help to avoid assumptions or unnecessary conflict by ensuring views are aired and tested.

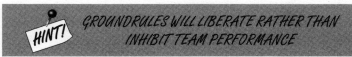

HINT! *GROUNDRULES WILL LIBERATE RATHER THAN INHIBIT TEAM PERFORMANCE*

The First Meeting

What it is

The project team should meet as soon as possible, once team members have been identified. At this first meeting it is helpful to:

- get members to introduce themselves
- create a relaxed, friendly and open atmosphere
- use an ice breaker exercise if appropriate
- discuss in detail:
  - the project goals and contract
  - the project plan
  - reporting and communication processes
  - roles and responsibilities.

The first two or three meetings of a newly formed team are critical for setting the tone. There is serious work at hand, but everyone can have fun and contribute to the team by working together. This requires a balance between learning about the task and learning about each other.

This tool outlines an agenda for the first meeting.

How to use it

1. Review the model agenda.
2. Adapt it to fit the needs of your team.
3. Agree who is going to lead each item and the time available.
4. Prepare any notes, visuals, handouts, etc required to support your items.

Model agenda for first meeting

1. Explain the goals of the meeting (2 minutes)

2. Review the agenda (2 minutes)

3. Make personal introductions (5 minutes)

4. Explain the roles of sponsor, team leader, team member, facilitator (5 minutes)

5. Review the brief from your team sponsor (5 minutes)

6. Agree groundrules/housekeeping as to how you want to work together (5 minutes)

7. Revisit some of the basic improvement tools as appropriate to your topic, eg:

- customer-supplier chains/processes
- Plan-Do-Check-Act improvement cycle
- effective teamwork. (10 minutes)

8. Start work on the improvement topic, eg:

- agree objectives
- agree overall plan
- identify customer requirements
- define current situation. (30 minutes)

9. Prepare for the next meeting:

- what needs to be done before next meeting
- draft agenda
- roles
- date, time, venue. (5 minutes)

10. Review meeting:

- seek feedback
- discuss how to make the next meeting better. (5 minutes)

11. Close: (2 minutes)

- thank people for contributions
- point the way ahead. *Total time: 1-1¹/₂ hours*

How it helps

It is important to get a new team off to a good start by running a well organised, enjoyable meeting. This tool gives an agenda which, when used with the effective meetings guidelines, should lead to this outcome.

YOU NEVER GET A SECOND CHANCE TO CREATE A FIRST IMPRESSION

The Team Contract

What it is

The team contract is:

- a short written document outlining the terms of reference
- agreed by all players
- open to renegotiation if circumstances change.

This tool outlines the context of an ideal contract and suggests a process for developing it.

How to use it

1. Review the model team contract on the next page and note the headings which apply to your team.

2. Under each heading note the information which is already agreed. Draft any additional points you feel are needed.

3. Review the draft contract with your sponsor to test your ideas and develop it further. It may be hard to be specific at this stage before you have done any detailed data gathering or analysis.

4. Present the draft contract at your first team meeting for discussion, improvement and agreement.

5. Circulate the amended draft to all members for final agreement.

6. Ensure the contract remains visible, appropriate and is applied throughout the project.

Model team contracts

✔ Team mission statement:
- the overall purpose or goal of the team
- how the team will contribute to the overall business goals
- a clear, simple and memorable statement that means something to those involved ☐

✔ Specific objectives:
- what outcomes are expected
- how success will be measured, eg what is it to produce? ☐

✔ Boundaries:
- what is/is not included in the project
- budget restrictions
- process start and finish points
- authorisation levels
- time limits on involvement or length of meetings
- sites/products/departments to be included ☐

✔ Contacts:
- who is likely to be contacted or involved during the project (beyond the team itself)
- will the team be involving external customers or suppliers ☐

✔ Timeframes:
- start and finish times
- milestones along the way eg for presenting proposals ☐

✔ Resources:
- time
- people
- budget
- access to specialist help
- cover for normal work ☐

✔ Roles:
- who's doing what ☐

How it helps

A team contract ensures everyone is clear about what has to be achieved within agreed resources.

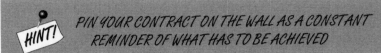

HINT!

PIN YOUR CONTRACT ON THE WALL AS A CONSTANT REMINDER OF WHAT HAS TO BE ACHIEVED

Checklist for Getting Started

What it is

This tool gives an overall checklist of issues that need to be discussed and resolved by the sponsor, the team leader and the team before beginning detailed work. It ensures the team is built on strong foundations.

How to use it

1. Review the checklist.

2. Tick off each point as you resolve it and keep separate notes on what you agree.

3. Once you can answer all of those questions you are ready to begin work in earnest in your team:

✔ What process or area for improvement will the team study?

✔ Why is this topic important?

✔ Are there other teams working on related topics that this team should coordinate with?

✔ What are the goals/objectives?

✔ How will success be measured?

✔ Who is the team sponsor?

✔ Who is the team leader?

✔ Is there a facilitator? If so, who?

✔ What skills/experience are required within the team and to what level? The three categories of skills and experience which need to be covered are:

- functional/technical

- problem solving/decision-making

- interpersonal.

✔ Bearing the last point in mind, who should be in the team? Are these people willing to give the time and to learn and develop the skills to be effective as a team?

✔ Is there power to take action?

✔ When, where, how often and for how long will the team meet?

✔ How often and in what format will the team report to its sponsor?

✔ When will the project begin and what is the target date for completion?

✔ What resources, eg money, equipment, facilities, etc will the team need?

✔ What training, if any, does the team need and how will it be provided?

✔ What in-house 'specialists' may need to get involved?

✔ How will team members' normal work be covered?

How it helps

This checklist ensures that the team is clear on the objectives and boundaries of the project and that all logistical and team membership issues have been considered before work commences. It can provide a framework for discussion in the early stages.

3 | Build the team

Stages of Team Growth*

What it is

Team growth is a gradual process. While there is some risk in being overly analytical in looking at typical team behaviours, there do seem to be some quite predictable stages through which many new teams go. One simple and effective way of looking at team development is to see it as four stages:

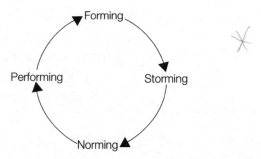

During each stage individuals in the team may look at both the team and the task in ways which reflect the differing and conflicting pressures they are under, as they gradually learn to adapt to this new way of doing things.

The team leader needs to recognise when the team has reached each stage and use the suggested team leader behaviours to help the team to continue to work effectively.

Team members need to understand at the start that 'ups and downs' are needed and inevitable – but will need careful handling!

* Developed from the original ideas of Bruce W. Tuckman

How to use it

1. Review the following descriptions of the four stages.

2. Decide what stage your team has reached.

3. Identify actions you can take to *either* get through your current stage as quickly as possible *or* maintain your team at the performing stage.

4. If you are about to set up a new team, use the tool to identify actions you can take to move through the first three stages as quickly as possible.

Stage 1: Forming

When a team first comes together, the team members need to explore and define acceptable group behaviour. It's a transition stage, from individual to team member status. It is also the time when some members will *test* the leader – *how far will he/she let us go?*

Don't be surprised if you see some, or all, of the following:

- Attempts to define, or redefine, the task and how it will be accomplished.

- Attempts to determine acceptable group behaviour and how to deal with group problems.

- Decisions on what information needs to be gathered.

- Abstract discussions of concepts and issues; or, for some members, impatience with these discussions.

- Discussion of things not really relevant to the task.

- Complaints about the organisation and perceived barriers to the task.

All of this is perfectly normal at this time – although you may feel that the team is accomplishing very little, the team does need to learn how to work together, and to *clear the air* on one or two issues.

Helpful team leader behaviours:

✔ Provide structure by holding regular meetings and assisting in task and role clarification

- ✔ Encourage participation by all, domination by none
- ✔ Facilitate learning about one another's areas of expertise and preferred working methods
- ✔ Share all relevant information
- ✔ Encourage members to ask questions of you and one another
- ✔ Agree ground rules
- ✔ Use team building exercises.

Stage 2: Storming

Storming is probably the most difficult stage for the team. They begin to realise that the task is different and more difficult than they imagined. Some members can become testy, blaming others in the team for small errors, others may become more pushy and over-zealous. Some may push their past experience, resisting any need for collaborating with other team members.

Don't be surprised to see these behaviours:

- Arguing amongst members, even when they agree on the central issue.
- Defensiveness and competition.
- Questioning the wisdom of those who selected the project and *this team.*
- Establishing unrealistic goals and concern about excessive work.
- Incidents of disunity, obvious tension and even jealousy.

Even now you may feel that the team is making little progress – but they are getting to know each other better and to understand each other's concerns and points of view.

Helpful team leader behaviours:

- ✔ Encourage joint problem solving; have members give reasons why an idea is useful and how to improve it
- ✔ Encourage the expression of different viewpoints

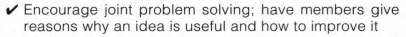

> ✔ Discuss the group's decision-making process and share decision-making responsibility appropriately
>
> ✔ Encourage members to state how they feel as well as what they think when they obviously have feelings about an issue
>
> ✔ Provide group members with the resources needed to do their jobs, as far as possible (when this is not possible, explain why)

Stage 3: Norming

It's at this stage that the team realises that they can complete the task and *achieve*. Team members find that they can accept the other team members, conflicts reduce and the groundrules are seen as important and realistic. Cooperation begins.

Don't be surprised to see these behaviours:

* more friendliness, discussion of the team's approaches, confiding in each other

* a common spirit and sense of purpose

* maintaining the groundrules and any defined boundaries (the *norms*).

Since the team members have now learned how to work together, and how to work out their differences, more time and energy will be devoted to the task. Significant progress can be seen.

> ### Helpful team leader behaviours:
>
> ✔ Talk openly about your own issues and concerns
>
> ✔ Have group members manage agenda items
>
> ✔ Give and request both positive and constructive negative feedback in the group
>
> ✔ Assign challenging problems for consensus decisions . (eg budget allocations)
>
> ✔ Delegate as much as the members are capable of handling; help them as necessary

Stage 4: Performing

By this stage the team has really settled down to the task. They have discovered the strengths and weaknesses of the team, and the roles that each can play productively.

You will probably observe these behaviours:

- Constructive *self-change*
- Closer attachment to the team
- An ability to work openly through team problems
- Interdependency and sharing of skills and experience.

Helpful team leader behaviours:

✔ Jointly set goals that are challenging

✔ Look for new opportunities to increase the group's scope

✔ Question assumptions and traditional ways of behaving

✔ Develop mechanisms for ongoing review by the group

✔ Recognise each member's contribution

✔ Develop members to their fullest potential through task assignments and feedback.

How it helps

The duration and intensity of these stages vary from team to team. Sometimes Stage 4 – performing – is achieved in a meeting or two. Other times it may take months to get there. Understanding these common patterns of growth will help a team leader not to overreact to normal problems or set unrealistic expectations that can only lead to frustration.

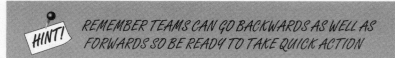

HINT! REMEMBER TEAMS CAN GO BACKWARDS AS WELL AS FORWARDS SO BE READY TO TAKE QUICK ACTION

Team Performance Curve

What it is

All teams experience highs and lows over time. The team performance curve is simply an illustration of some of the causes of these highs and lows. It can be used to manage the expectations, both of the team members and those outside of the team, of what it will actually feel like to be part of the team.

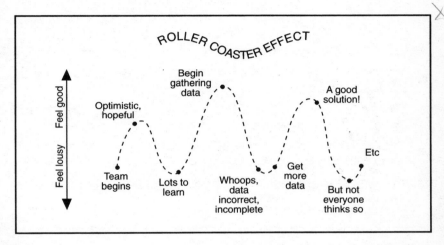

The performance curve illustrates the way teams frequently experience fluctuations in mood, depending upon how well they appear to be going. With every step forward, the future looks bright and team members are optimistic. But progress is rarely smooth. As things go wrong, and as progress swings from forward to stalled, and from stalled to backwards, the team mood will swing too.

Teams often begin feeling optimistic and hopeful, but become impatient when the project is underway and they realise how much they have to learn about improvement.

When they begin collecting data, team members again feel encouraged – at last they are making progress. But then the mood can swing again if they realise that the data collection methods were wrong, or incomplete, and they've got to go back and get some more.

Then, there is the elation of finding a workable, even elegant solution to the problem. There can be a let-down when resistance to the proposed change is met – from the boss, or worse, colleagues who work in the affected area.

How to use it

1. The best way to use this cycle is to understand it and accept it with a 'this too shall pass' attitude. Changes in attitude, just like growth stages, are normal. The team must cultivate patience, while not losing its sense of urgency.

2. However, there are actions you can take to minimise the lows:

Practical steps to take to minimise the lows include:

✔ regular and balanced reviews of performance

✔ being open about feeling 'down'

✔ re-focusing on the goals and/or progress to date

✔ recognition of achievements

✔ reminders that this is 'normal'

✔ cutting short meetings or having breaks if the team is starting to wallow

✔ trying a new tool or method to re-stimulate interest

✔ sharing the experiences of others who have been through the same lows (and come out of them!)

Eventually, everyone will understand how projects unfold and will be able to set a realistic pace for the project.

This roller-coaster effect is on a relatively short time frame overlying the overall stages of team growth (after Tuckman) described earlier in this Toolbox.

How it helps

As team leader you can use this curve to explain to a 'down' team that the stage they have reached is part of a normal up and down sequence of team working. You can use the communication tools discussed later in this Toolbox to discuss feelings and plan action.

DON'T PANIC IF THINGS SEEM LOW — IT'S NORMAL!
FOCUS YOUR ENERGY ON MOVING UP AGAIN

Teambuilding or Warm-up Exercises

What they are

Short enjoyable exercises to be used at the beginning of meetings to re-energise and focus team members.

How to use them

1. There are many types of team building exercise. You must choose the most appropriate for your team, given:

- their needs and objectives
- the stage of development of the team
- team size
- time available.

2. The following list gives some suggestions. Use these as a starting point but don't be afraid to be creative and design your own!

 TEAM BUILDING EXERCISES ARE AN OPPORTUNITY TO TAKE SMALL RISKS

Examples

✔ **Introductions:**

- to the whole group/in pairs
- using personal data - role/experience/ circumstances, etc

✔ **Analogies:**

- have fun identifying the most appropriate animals/ vehicles/instruments/flowers, etc to describe themselves/each other

- ✔ **Pictures:**
  - – draw selves/each other/team/division/company, etc
  - – use flip charts and lots of colour
- ✔ **Choose specific piece of personal data and share them,** eg:
  - – most embarrassing moments
  - – main achievements
  - – secrets
- ✔ **Have a fun brainstorm,** eg 100 uses for a baked bean tin
- ✔ **Superlatives:** have a quick quiz on who's tallest, heaviest, oldest, baldest, etc
- ✔ **Share hopes, fears and concerns** for the team/ the project
- ✔ **Share individual wants** from the team/project
- ✔ **Share values** in terms of what is most important to you/what drives you
- ✔ **Group conversations.** Throw in an opening line such as:

  - – I would like to be ......
  - – Nothing is so frustrating as .....
  - – If I were chairman I would .....
  - – If you want to annoy me ....
  - – A rewarding job is one that ......

- ✔ **Draw process maps** of own jobs/sections/office and share them
- ✔ **Use a problem solving tool,** eg Forcefield Analysis/ Cause and Effect Analysis to identify how to improve the level of team performance

✔ **Choose a name for the team**

✔ **Search for common denominators,** eg identify pairs who have something in common that's different to the rest of the group

✔ **Brainstorm** and discuss barriers to performance

✔ **Complete a task,** eg constructing a model or developing a plan, to test and improve the team's skills at planning and working together

3. Always spend a few minutes reviewing the exercises used to draw out reactions and learning points.

How they help

These exercises will help teams:

- switch-off the everyday things buzzing around at the start of the meeting.

- get into the right frame of mind for the session.

- get to know each other better.

- break down barriers.

- improve team performance.

4 | Work together

How to be a Good Team Leader

What it is

A checklist for team leaders to consider their own leadership behaviour.

How to use it

1. Review the checklist.

2. Assess your behaviour honestly against the criteria.

3. Resolve to take action on any area you feel could be improved.

An effective team leader will use the GRIPS model

Define **G**oals:

✔ help the team and each individual to be clear about who their customer is, what outputs are required from them and the standards they need to meet

✔ identify and agree objectives for continuous improvement

✔ demonstrate how these objectives contribute to the overall corporate goal(s)

Clarify **R**oles:

✔ identify how each individual fits into the team and the customer-supplier chain(s)

✔ explain your role and how you will provide support

Strive for honest **I**nteraction:

✔ swap constructive feedback; listen to your team

✔ share feelings and concerns; be open

✔ aim for equality not dominance

✔ admit mistakes; give praise as well as censure

Support **P**ersonal development:

✔ systematically identify individual's strengths and needs

✔ agree personal development goals

✔ identify ways to meet these needs and goals

✔ coach, counsel and facilitate personal development

Adapt your **S**tyle:

✔ use the appropriate style to reflect each individual's level of development and the nature of the task. For example:

- • use TELL when someone is very unsure or lacking knowledge and experience

- • try CONSULTING your team to gain their views and ideas before you make a decision

- • when they have more experience, build their confidence by JOINT decision-making

- • when individuals and/or the team have sufficient experience and confidence then DELEGATE goals and task to them and let them be responsible for working out how to achieve them

How it helps

Effective leadership is one of the key factors in successful teams. This **GRIPS** checklist summarises the main things a team leader needs to work on.

How to be a Good Team Member

What it is

An effective leader alone is not enough to make a team work well. Each individual must make a contribution. This checklist outlines the main areas that this should cover.

How to use it

1. Review the checklist.

2. Identify or seek feedback on those areas which you feel you already deliver.

3. Identify the points you need to work on.

4. Develop an action plan to improve your contribution.

An effective team member:

✔ Knows and understands the purpose, objectives and performance measures of the team

✔ Contributes constructively to the development of the objectives and measures and plans to achieve them

✔ Has individual objectives and tasks to complete to contribute towards the team performance

✔ Attends team meetings; punctually and willingly

✔ Contributes ideas, information and experience during the meetings

✔ Takes an active role (scribe, timekeeper, etc) in meetings as required

✔ Listens to other members and builds on their views and ideas

✔ Participates constructively in debate

✔ Accepts the consensus view of the team

✔ Takes a share of the work to be done between meetings and completes this to a high standard on time

✔ Supports the leader and other members outside the team once plans and actions have been agreed

✔ Inputs high energy and enthusiasm into the team and the work to be done

✔ Recognises the contributions and help of others in the team.

How it helps

This checklist details the behaviours and attitudes of an effective team member. It can be used to clarify expectations, review performance and develop individuals. It develops the role description of a team member given earlier in the Toolbox.

Belbin Team Roles

What it is

Meredith Belbin described 9 team roles which are evident in successful teams (NB: individuals can take more than one role; teams do not have to have nine members!).

These roles are not 'jobs' which can be picked up or put down; they reflect the personality and competencies of individuals and are often assumed unconsciously.

This tool describes the roles and gives a method for using them to review and improve team performance.

How to use it

1. Review the role descriptions.

2. Identify examples of the roles being taken in your team.

3. Identify the gaps, ie any roles that appear to be missing in your team.

4. Identify what you can do to 'plug' these gaps – either by developing skills within the team or bringing in new members.

Belbin team roles

Chairman/Coordinator

Controls the way the team moves forward. Ensures the team members' efforts and strengths are put to good use.

Shaper

Gets the team to look at where it is going – its objectives and priorities. Tries to keep the team activity focused.

Company Worker/Implementer

Gets practical action going. Turns the ideas and plans into practical tasks that people can actually get on with. Is systematic and methodical.

Completer/Finisher

Checks the details, ensuring nothing is overlooked and no mistakes made. Keeps an eye on time, deadlines and accuracy. Gives the team a sense of urgency.

Innovator/Plant

Suggests new ideas and creative solutions. Identifies new opportunities. Sees problems or setbacks as opportunities. Suggests new ways of operating.

Monitor/Evaluator

Evaluates ideas objectively to see if they are realistic and profitable. Can interpret and evaluate complex issues.

Resource Investigator

Keeps the team in touch with what is happening outside the team. Learns about ideas, information, developments and new possibilities in the outside world.

Team Worker

Encourages others, helps others out, is sensitive to people's needs and feelings.

Specialist

Has specialist knowledge or experience to contribute to the team, eg IT, legal, having previously worked on a relevant project elsewhere etc.

How it helps

Belbin team roles can be used to explain and address 'gaps' in teams that impair performance. Questionnaires are available that allow the identification of the typical, natural roles performed by individuals when in a team. These can be used to assemble balanced teams as well as analysing existing ones.

LOOK FOR A RANGE OF ROLES IN A TEAM
— TOO MANY THE SAME, LEADS
TO UNNECESSARY CONFLICT

Communication Skills: Listen Actively

What it is

Active Listening means listening beyond just the words, to obtain their real meaning.

How to use it

1. Quieten your own mind

- Put aside other matters and concerns.
- Do not interrupt.
- Do not finish other people's sentences.
- Breath calmly and deeply.

2. Control the environment

- Shut out background noise as much as possible.
- Stop interruptions.
- Remove physical barriers.
- Get fairly close to the speaker.
- Don't invade their personal space.

3. Listen carefully to what is being said

- Focus on the speaker.
- Shut out your thoughts and reactions.
- Give the speaker your full, unbiased attention.

4. Use positive non-verbal signals

- Nodding.
- Smiling.
- Attentive posture.
- Interested facial expression.
- Eye contact.

5. Use positive verbal signals

- "Good idea".
- "I like that".

- "I hadn't thought of that before".
- "Interesting".
- Prompting (repeating the speaker's most significant words or phrases).

6. Use pauses
- Spaces are natural.
- Don't try and fill the silence.
- Allow time for absorption and reflection.
- Don't rush or hurry the speaker unnecessarily.
- Relax.

7. Summarise
Restate your understanding of the content and/or reflect feelings. Use the speaker's most significant words.
- "Let me check to make sure I understood ..."
- "You're saying that .."
- "As I understand you ..."
- "Let me see if I've got that. The goal for this session is ..".

8. Avoid unhelpful behaviour
- Don't doodle.
- Don't stare or look aggressive.
- Don't hide behind a barrier.
- Don't keep looking at your watch.

How it helps

Listening Actively ensures you really focus on the other person's views, ideas and feelings and helps to ensure true two-way communication.

 HINT!

YOU HAVE TWO EARS AND ONE MOUTH
– USE THEM IN THOSE PROPORTIONS

Communication Skills: Ask Questions

What it is

Questions are used to draw out information from others.

How to use it

There are several types of questions. Choose the most appropriate:

1. Open-ended questions

Open questions promote discovery and stimulate thinking. They are useful to help the other person start talking about a topic, outline a situation, give a broad description of what happened and how he or she reacted.

There are three broad types of open question:

- **Clarifying questions**
  - "What specifically does that mean to you?"
  - "Can I make sure I understand that ...?"
  - "If I hear correctly, what you are saying is ..."

- **Creative questions**
  - "How have you seen others handle similar situations?"
  - "What do you think about...?"
  - "Would you like to talk more about it?"
  - "I'd be interested in hearing more"
  - "What would be your approach if there were no constraints?"

- **Process questions**
  - "What would you like to get from this session?"
  - "What do I need to communicate to ensure everyone understands your role?"
  - "What authority do you think you need to complete this task?"

2. Follow-up or probing questions

The purpose of follow-up questions is to get information, broaden decisions and understand reasons and motivations. Do not over use 'why'. It causes people to become defensive.

- "In what way would this help achieve greater customer satisfaction?"

- "What other aspects of this should be considered?"

- "How would you involve others in accomplishing this plan?"

Follow-up questions are useful for probing – getting to the heart of a topic, checking information and filling in detail.

A particular type of follow-up question is the reflective question, useful for gaining a clearer understanding, revealing more information or uncovering feelings.

- "You say you were pleased..."

- "Incompetent...?"

- "You say he reacted to this. How did he react...?"

3. Closed questions

Closed questions are those that lead to either 'yes' or 'no'. They are useful in checking facts quickly but can lead to a one-sided conversation. Examples are:

- 'Have you been shopping recently?'
- 'Is there enough money in the bank?'
- 'Have you done this sort of work before?'

A closed question can be a useful lead into open questions once an area to explore has been identified.

4. Less useful questions

Certain types of questions are less useful. Try not to use them – these include:

- leading questions ("I assume you...").
- hypothetical questions ("If you were in my place...").
- multiple questions.

*I HAVE SIX GOOD FRIENDS AND TRUE,
THEY TAUGHT ME ALL I KNEW.
THEIR NAMES ARE WHAT AND WHEN AND HOW
AND WHY AND WHERE AND WHO*

R KIPLING

5. The Questioning Funnel

Questions can be most effective when used in series to gather information. The funnel illustrates how:

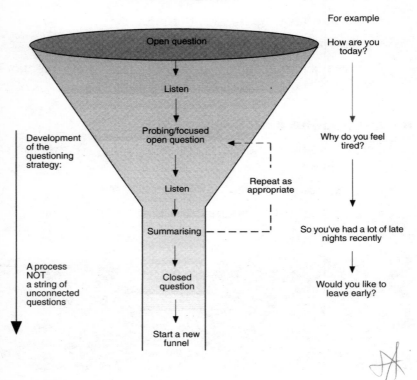

The Questioning Funnel

How it helps

Questions are the only way to seek information and to fully involve an individual. Along with listening they ensure two-way communication.

Communication Skills: Give and Receive Feedback

What it is

Feedback is a way of learning more about ourselves and the effect our behaviour has on others.

You may be called upon to give feedback to an improvement team or to individuals within it. You must also be able to receive feedback from others working with you on improvement initiatives.

Constructive feedback increases self-awareness, offers options and encourages development, so it can be important to learn to give it and receive it. Constructive feedback does not mean only positive feedback. Negative feedback, given skilfully, can be very important and useful.

Destructive feedback is given in an unskilled way, leaving the recipient simply feeling bad with seemingly nothing on which to build or options for using the learning.

How to give feedback

1. Start with the positive

Most people need encouragement, to be told when they are doing something well. When offering feedback it can really help the receiver to hear first what you like about them or what they have done well.

For example, "I really like how well you listened to Jim, however on that occasion I did feel you made an assumption about him, without checking it out".

It is easy to put the focus on mistakes more often than strengths. In a rush to criticise we may overlook the things we liked. If the positive is registered first, any negative is more likely to be listened to and acted upon.

2. Be specific

Try to avoid general comments which are not very useful when it comes to developing skills. Statements such as "You were brilliant!" or "It was awful" may be pleasant or dreadful to hear, but they do not give enough detail to be useful sources of learning. Try to pinpoint what the person did which led you to use the label "brilliant" or "awful", eg "The way you asked that question just at that moment was really helpful" or "At that moment you seemed to be imposing your values on the other person". Specific feedback gives more opportunity for learning.

3. Refer to behaviour which can be changed

It is not likely to be helpful to give a person feedback about something over which they have no choice.eg "I really don't like your face/your height/the fact that you are bald etc" is not offering information about which a person can do very much. On the other hand to be told that "It would help me if you smiled more or looked at me when you speak" can give the person something on which to work.

4. Offer alternatives

If you do offer negative feedback then do not simply criticise, but suggest what the person could have done differently. Turn the negative into a positive suggestion, eg "The fact that you remained seated when Anne came in seemed unwelcoming. I think if you had walked over and greeted her it would have helped to put her at ease".

5. Be descriptive rather than evaluative

Tell the person what you saw or heard and the effect it had on you, rather than merely something was "good, bad, etc", eg "Your tone of voice as you said that really made me feel that you were concerned" is likely to be more useful than "That was good".

6. Own the feedback

It can be easy to say to the other person "You are........". suggesting that you are offering a universally agreed opinion about that person. In fact all we are entitled to give is our own experience of that person at a particular time. It is also important that we take responsibility for the feedback we offer. Beginning the feedback with "I" or "in my opinion", is a way of avoiding the impression of being the giver of "cosmic judgements" about the other person.

7. Leave the recipient with a choice

Feedback which demands change or is imposed heavily on the other person can raise resistance. Feedback does not involve telling somebody how they must be to suit us. Skilled feedback offers people information about themselves in a way which leaves them with a choice about whether to act on it or not. It can help to examine the consequences of any decision to change or not to change, but do not prescribe change.

8. Think what it says about you

Feedback is likely to say as much about the giver as the receiver. It will say a good deal about your values, and what you focus on in others. Therefore we can learn about ourselves if we listen to the feedback we give others.

Checklist for giving feedback:

✔ Start with the positive

✔ Be specific

✔ Refer to behaviour that can be changed

✔ Offer alternatives

✔ Be descriptive rather than evaluative

✔ Own the feedback

✔ Leave the recipient with a choice

✔ Think what it says about you

How to receive feedback

If we are on the receiving end of feedback we can help ourselves by encouraging the giver to use some of the skills above, and to:

1. Listen to the feedback rather than immediately rejecting or arguing with it

Feedback can be uncomfortable to hear, but we may be poorer without it. People may think things without telling us and then we may be at a disadvantage.Remember that people do have their opinions about you and will have their perceptions of your behaviour, and it can help to be aware of those. However, do remember that you are also entitled to your opinion and you may choose to ignore it as being of little significance, irrelevant, or referring to behaviour which for some other reason you wish to maintain. Nevertheless, breathe deeply, stay calm and listen carefully!

2. Be clear about what is being said

Try to avoid jumping to conclusions or becoming immediately defensive. If you do, people may cut down their feedback or may not be able to use it fully. Make sure you understand the feedback before you respond to it. Ask for examples if it is vague.

A useful technique can be to paraphrase or repeat the criticism, to check that you have understood. Acknowledge any valid points even if there are things you don't agree with.

3. Check it out with others rather than relying on only one source

If we rely on one source then we may imagine that the individual's opinion is shared by everybody. In fact, if we check out with others we may find that others experience us differently and we will have a more balanced view of ourselves which can keep the feedback in proportion.

4. Ask for the feedback you want but don't get

Feedback can be so important that we may have to ask for it if it does not occur naturally. Sometimes we do get feedback but it is restricted to one aspect of our behaviour and we may have to request feedback we would find useful but do not get.

5. Decide what you will do as a result of the feedback

"It takes two to know one." Each of us needs to know how other people experience us to extend our self-awareness, which is incomplete if merely our own version of ourselves. So we can use feedback to help our own development.

When we receive it we can assess its value; the consequences of ignoring it or using it, and finally decide what we will do as a result of it.

If we do not take decisions on the basis of it then it can be wasted.

Checklist for receiving feedback:

✔ Listen to feedback – don't reject or argue with it

✔ Be clear about what is being said

✔ Check it out with others rather than relying on only one source

✔ Ask for feedback you want but don't get

✔ Decide what you will do as a result of the feedback.

How it helps

By seeking or providing constructive, specific feedback you ensure a realistic perception of current performance which is the first step towards personal and team improvement.

ACCURATE FEEDBACK IS THE STARTING POINT FOR SELF-DEVELOPMENT

Participate in Meetings

What it is

If you haven't had much experience or practice, participating in meetings (either by presenting information or contributing to discussions) can be daunting. This tool gives some practical tips to help you participate effectively.

How to use it

Use the following checklists to make sure you are ready and prepared:

Prepare your input

If you are asked to present some information:

✔ Be clear what you want to achieve – get a decision seek ideas or views/transfer information, etc

✔ Decide what information you need to get across facts/figures/opinions/ideas, etc

✔ Put the information into a clear, logical order

✔ Take account of who will be there and what they already know to pitch the level of your input

✔ Prepare any visuals – flips, overheads, screens, samples, etc and make sure you are comfortable about how to use them

✔ Decide if you need to prepare any supporting notes and if these should be circulated in advance

✔ Structure your input – introduction, 'meat', conclusions, recommendations

✔ Anticipate likely questions or contentious issues and how you will handle them

✔ Check you have sufficient time to do what you need to do at the meeting. If not, either amend your input or negotiate more time.

Manage your input

During your presentation or discussion:

✔ Draw people in to comment or answer questions, so the spotlight is not entirely on you

✔ Explain any jargon that may be unfamiliar to some people

✔ Say if you don't know or get muddled – your team will be with you!

✔ Make lots of eye contact to keep everyone interested

✔ Be brief, don't ramble; keep focused on your goal

✔ Be sure to talk loud enough so everyone can hear; stand up if it helps

Contribute effectively

If you are involved in a team discussion or debate:

✔ Listen carefully to other views and ideas, don't spend all your time planning what you want to say

✔ Support and build on good ideas; don't put them down just because someone else thought of them or you're not sure how they would work

✔ Don't talk over others; they won't be listening; say 'can I just say something…' and wait for silence

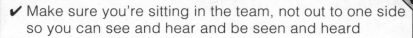

✔ Make sure you're sitting in the team, not out to one side so you can see and hear and be seen and heard

✔ Input your views, experience, ideas as appropriate

✔ Be clear, brief and to the point and then say 'would you like more detail?/can I develop it further?'

✔ Question and constructively challenge others if they are unclear or appear illogical or irrelevant but don't be sarcastic – it's probably you who's confused!

✔ Get more actively involved by offering to scribe/keep notes/act as timekeeper. These jobs can increase your visibility and influence

✔ Suggest tools that might help the team to be more effective and get everyone involved.

RELAX! TRY AND FOCUS ON THE TEAM RATHER THAN YOURSELF

How it helps

Teams can be expensive. It is therefore important that everyone involved contributes effectively. This tool gives practical tips on how to contribute as a presenter or during less formal discussions.

Focus Group Thinking:

Six Thinking Hats (De Bono)

What it is

The **six hats** is a general thinking framework which replaces the adversarial thinking of argument and the drift of discussion with constructive parallel thinking. At any moment everyone is thinking in the same direction.

The hats may be used systematically in a sequence but can also be used singly as a symbolic way of requesting a particular type of thinking.

The hats have been shown to reduce meeting times to one quarter of their usual length and to increase thinking productivity by up to five fold.

The hats are:

White: (paper) Focus on information. What is available. What is needed. How to get it. Both hard information and soft information.

Red: (fire) Permission to express intuition, feelings and emotion.

Black: (judges' robes) Caution. Risk assessment. Potential problems. Downside. Critical and looking at why something does not fit budget, policy, ethics, etc.

Yellow: (sunshine) Focus on benefits and values and ways to make something work.

Green: (vegetation) Everyone seeks to be creative: new ideas, alternatives, possibilities, variations on an idea.

Blue: (sky and overview) Control and management of the thinking process. Defining the problem. Summary, outcome and decision.

How it's done

1. Proper training is recommended.

2. The sequence of hats is determined under the initial blue hat.

3. Everyone wears the same hat at the same time.

4. Decisions, outcomes and next steps are determined under the final blue hat.

How it helps

Speeds up thinking very considerably. Framework for constructive and design thinking. Uses full intelligence and experience of all those taking part. Evaluation is an integral part of the process and decisions usually make themselves by the end of the session. The hats mimic the change in brain chemistry for different modes of thinking.

Coaching

What it is

Coaching is a process by which a team leader or fellow team member through direct discussion, questioning and guided activities, helps a person to do a task better than would otherwise have been the case. It helps to achieve both performance improvement and individual development. It deals with the knowledge, skills, competence and confidence needed to perform specific tasks in real work situations.

How to use it

The coaching process consists of a number of key stages. To coach effectively you need to follow each of the stages in this checklist:

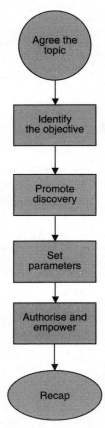

1. Agree the topic

- What is the topic/project you would like to delegate and coach another individual to do? Agree this with the person concerned.

2. Identify the objectives

- What is your long term objective? eg "In six weeks I'll have put forward costed recommendations for moving the office to Manchester". Discuss and agree this, ensuring that it is a SMART objective.

- What would you like to learn/gain from each coaching session?

- How long do you think you will both need to achieve this?

3. Promote discovery – the current position

- What is the present situation?

- What has been done already?

- What happened as a result of that?

- What evidence is there that this problem exists?

- Who else has this experience?

- Where exactly does the problem lie?

- When does this problem occur?

- Who else is involved/responsible?

- How do they see the situation?

4. Promote discovery – the options

Ask your coachee to come up with a number of options and encourage him to evaluate the consequences of adopting each one. Ask him:

- What would be the consequences for eg staffing, budget, other departments?

- How have others tackled this in the past?

- Which option do you think is most viable?

5. Set parameters

Establish exactly what needs to be done and by when. Ensure the coachee knows how far he can go without reference to you – don't assume he understands.

6. Authorise and empower

Ensure that others know you have authorised your coachee to do the agreed work/research, otherwise they may quickly hit barriers to cooperation.

Ensure that they have the resources, eg transport, expenses and administrative support, to carry out their task.

7. Recap

At the end of each session agree with the following to ensure you both understand:

- What are the next steps?
- What steps are *you* going to take?
- When will he do that?
- What are the obstacles?
- What could stop him achieving this?
- What support do you need?
- Who can he enlist to support him?

How it helps

Coaching helps achieve both performance improvement and employee development. It is an important tool in achieving empowerment, improving morale and releasing management time.

Make Decisions

What it is

An important task for teams is to make decisions. For example:

- What goals to tackle
- How to improve a process
- What data to collect
- Which options to implement.

There are many tools in the Quest *Solve that problem!* Toolbox which improve the quality of decision making in a team. This tool focuses on who should be involved.

How to use it

1. Clarify the decision to be made.

2. Review the spectrum of styles available to the team leader.

3. As leader decide which style is most appropriate in this case and brief the team.

4. Use *Solve that problem!* to identify possible tools that you and/or the team could use to make the decision.

5. Make the decision.

6. Review the success of your decision and the style used with the team in order to agree how to improve upon it next time.

The spectrum of decision making styles		
Style	**Action**	**Options**
Tell	you make the decision and tell the team	• simply announce it • explain the reasons/background
Consult	you get the team's opinion and make the decision	• ask them separately • ask them when together
Joint	you and part of the team make the decision	• choose the most appropriate people • use those available at the time • you act as another team member • canvass majority view • aim for consensus
Delegate	you delegate the decision to the team	• pass over to part of team • pass over to whole team

The following factors should be taken into account when choosing a style:

✔ Who has relevant experience/knowledge to contribute

✔ How much time is available

✔ The importance of gaining real commitment

✔ How creative the decision needs to be

✔ The significance of the decision – routine or strategic

✔ The development need of the team to improve its decision-making

✔ The value of widening the perspectives/understanding of individuals

✔ The need to build trust and confidence with the team

✔ How much control you are prepared to relinquish.

Irrespective of the decision-making style, it is important to achieve a feeling of commitment to the decision. The strongest commitment is achieved through **consensus reaching**.

In order to reach consensus you need to:

✔ Listen to what others are saying

✔ Build on others ideas, not knock them down

✔ Periodically summarise where you are

✔ Ensure quieter members have a say

✔ Look for tension points and state feelings

✔ Check what people think/how they feel about ideas

✔ Don't take silence for consent

✔ Make proposals and seek either agreement or objections

✔ Look for common ground and build on it until differences are marginalised.

How it helps

A fallacy of teams is that everyone should be involved in every decision. This tool outlines a range of styles which can be used and gives some tips on when each is appropriate. Used appropriately it will improve the decision–making within the team.

TEAMS THAT AVOID DECISIONS ACHIEVE VERY LITTLE

Resolve Conflict

What it is

Conflict is inevitable within teams. It is not bad or harmful if handled correctly. In fact, it can lead to far greater creativity and innovation by challenging assumptions, values and proposals. This tool gives a method for handling such challenges in order to get to a collaborative win–win solution.

How to use it

1. Analyse why conflict is occurring

Here are some causes of conflict in teams:

- **Objectives:** The team's goal or objective is unclear or unacceptable to one or more members of the team.

- **Perception:** Some aspects of the task are interpreted based upon past experiences. These experiences influence the way in which the members of the team see themselves or the task. An example might be: 'Management will never go along with this solution (because) they never have done so in the past'.

- **Emotions:** Emotions can cloud judgement, confuse facts and feelings and get things out of proportion. (They are also a tremendous source of energy and morale, so should not be ignored!)

- **Communication:** The complexity of human communication, both verbal and non-verbal, always provides an opportunity for misinterpretation of meaning or intention.

2. **Present the issue unemotionally** – use an "I" message and ask for the other party's help. "I feel frustrated with your proposal – can we agree to work together on this? I really need your help."

3. **Clarify and define the issue**

   "Here's how I see the problem ... what do you think is the issue?"

4. **Understand the other person's position**

   - listen without judgement or rebuttal
   - ask for clarification (probe as needed), "can you tell me more about that?"

5. **Give your point of view**

   - use "I" statements – express it assertively and take ownership for it
   - test for understanding.

6. **Jointly develop an objective or condition on which both parties agree**

   - "What are we both after?"
   - "Under what conditions will we both be satisfied?"
   - "The problem will be solved when ... "

7. **Brainstorm alternatives**

   - put judgement on hold.

8. **Jointly choose one alternative as a tentative solution.**

9. **Jointly decide how each party will know if the solution is working.**

YOU ARE AFTER A WIN/WIN SITUATION – DON'T LET PEOPLE 'WIN' THE ARGUMENT AT THE EXPENSE OF OTHERS LOSING.

How it helps

This tool gives a process or method for handling conflict which helps to produce an effective outcome for both parties.

DON'T AVOID CONFLICT. HANDLED CONSTRUCTIVELY IT CAN LEAD TO CREATIVE INSIGHTS

Run Effective Meetings

What it is

An effective meeting is one in which the objectives have been clearly defined and are achieved in a timely manner with appropriate and positive contributions from everyone who is involved.

Effective meetings don't just happen. They require thought, planning, organisation and leadership. This tool gives checklists and proformas on the following:

- Pre-meeting preparation.

- Sample agenda.

- Helpful behaviour at the meeting.

- Groundrules for ensuring appropriate and positive contributions.

- Measuring meeting effectiveness.

- Sample meeting record.

- Things to do after the meeting.

- Sample meeting review proformas.

Pre-meeting preparation

✔ Clearly establish the purpose and objectives of the meeting.

✔ Consider whether a meeting is actually necessary. Could the objective be achieved more effectively using other methods eg memo, E-mail, one-to-one discussions, conference calls, etc.

✔ Decide who needs to be involved, who should chair the meeting.

✔ Discuss the intended meeting with and brief those who are to be involved.

✔ Organise the date, time and place for the meeting.

✔ Prepare and issue an agenda which includes:

- items to be discussed
- the time allocated to each item
- the name/initials of the person who will lead the discussion
- the date, start and finish times, location
- any appropriate attachments and pre-briefing materials.

✔ Organise the room, making arrangements for the following, as necessary:

- equipment, eg flip charts, OHP's, whiteboards
- paper, pens, pencils
- appropriate seating and table layouts
- refreshments.

Arrange for one of the meeting participants to make meeting notes, or arrange a meeting secretary

Sample meeting record

Team: _____   Date: _____

Members present: _____

Visitors: _____

1. Subject/item _____
   Key points _____

Decisions	Action by (name)	Deadline (date/time)

2. Subject/item _____
   Key points _____

Decisions	Action by (name)	Deadline (date/time)

(Continue for all subjects.)

Date of next meeting: _____   date/time/location

HINT! LABEL ITEMS ON THE AGENDA FOR INFORMATION, FOR
DISCUSSION OR FOR DECISION AND HIGHLIGHT ANY
SPECIFIC OR UNUSUAL POINTS IN THE
ATTACHMENTS/NOTES SECTION

Helpful behaviour at the meeting

✔ Start on time

✔ Introduce anyone who is new to the group, or if it's a first meeting ask attendees to introduce themselves

✔ Review the purpose/objectives of the meeting. Check for understanding

✔ Use groundrules for ensuring appropriate and positive contributions

✔ Check understanding and agreement at regular points

✔ Record actions and decisions as they are agreed

✔ Try and ensure an even distribution of actions

✔ If important issues, outside the scope of the agenda are raised, capture them in a 'parking bay' for future discussion

✔ If agreement cannot be reached on a particular point either:

  • work back through the arguments to find a common point and then offer/suggest alternatives, or

  • establish the fundamental point of disagreement and take up the discussion again after the meeting with those concerned

✔ Keep track of time

✔ Review actions including: the statement of action required, who is responsible, and when the action should be completed by

✔ Agree time, date, location of the next meeting

✔ Review the meeting itself to identify areas for improvement at future meetings

MORE THAN ONE PERSON MAY BE INVOLVED IN COMPLETING AN ACTION, BUT ONLY ONE PERSON SHOULD BE NAMED AS BEING RESPONSIBLE FOR ENSURING ITS COMPLETION

Ground rules for ensuring appropriate and positive contributions

✔ Listen when others are speaking

✔ Understand what is being said, ask questions if unclear

✔ Respect opinions of others

✔ Value all contributions

✔ Build on suggestions or ideas, don't kill them

✔ Surface hidden agendas, be honest, show feels and concerns

✔ Be open minded, look for positives

✔ Don't get too emotional

✔ Don't dominate discussions...encourage others to express their views and opinions

✔ Stick to the point

✔ Have fun

You may also choose to measure certain aspects of your meeting effectiveness, for example:

✔ Percentage of actions complete on time

✔ Variations from start and finish times

✔ Lateness

✔ Over/under run on agenda items (especially useful for regular items as times can be adjusted accordingly)

✔ Timely production of agenda and meeting notes

✔ Feelings of attendees

Sample meeting record

Team: _____   Date: _____

Members present: _____

Visitors: _____

1. Subject/item _____

   Key points _____

Decisions	Action by (name)	Deadline (date/time)

2. Subject/item _____

   Key points _____

Decisions	Action by (name)	Deadline (date/time)

(Continue for all subjects.)

Date of next meeting: date/time/location

_____   _____

Things to do after the meeting

✔ Produce and issue the notes of actions agreed within 24 hours of the meeting

✔ Progress the completion of actions assigned

✔ Monitor the progress of actions

✔ Prepare for the next meeting

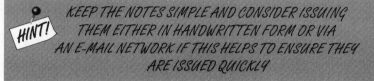

HINT! KEEP THE NOTES SIMPLE AND CONSIDER ISSUING THEM EITHER IN HANDWRITTEN FORM OR VIA AN E-MAIL NETWORK IF THIS HELPS TO ENSURE THEY ARE ISSUED QUICKLY

Sample meeting review proforma

Here are two examples of meeting review sheets:

Meeting review (1)

We all share responsibility for holding effective meetings. To help us improve, please record your impression of the effectiveness of this meeting:

	Weak	OK	Good	Brilliant
Our timing (punctual, clear time plan agreed, everything finished	[1]	[2]	[3]	[4]
Our discipline (kept to the brief, roles clear, used tools when appropriate)	[1]	[2]	[3]	[4]
Our dynamics (listening, supporting, not dominating or over-talking, openness	[1]	[2]	[3]	[4]
Our energy (all involved, enthusiastic, positive, fun	[1]	[2]	[3]	[4]
Our result (informative discussion, new ideas, valuable output, all agreed)	[1]	[2]	[3]	[4]

	Weak	OK	Good	Brilliant
Total				

out of 20

Meeting review (2)

We all share responsibility for holding effective meetings.
To help us improve, please record your views of this meeting on the form
below:

Effective Meeting Review

Meeting date: _____   Chair: _____
Name of meeting: _____

Checklist		Mark
Meeting objectives		
How necessary was the meeting?	0 - 10	
Were the objectives agreed at beginning of meeting?	0 - 5	
Were the objectives met?	0 - 15	
	Sub - total/30	☐
Meeting preparation		
Was agenda, with lead names for each item, objectives and prereading received three working days before meeting?	0 - 10	
Was full use made of sub-groups?	0 - 10	
	Sub - total/20	☐
Actions		
Were individual actions set, with deadlines?	0 - 5	
Were the individual actions and deadlines agreed?	0 - 10	
Were the actions completed from previous meeting?	0 - 10	
	Sub - total/25	☐
Time management		
Did the meeting start and finish on time?	0 - 10	
Was sufficient time allowed for priority items?	0 - 5	
Were all attendees present on time?		
Deduct 2 points/person late		
	Sub - total/15	☐
Attendees at meeting		
Were too many people present or attending the whole meeting unnecessarily?	0 - 5	
Did every attendee have a clear and necessary role and was any key contributor missing?	0 - 5	
	Sub - total/10	☐
	TOTAL/100	☐

How it helps

Meetings are a common feature of business life and can
occupy anything up to 40% of a manager's time.

Following these guidelines will help to ensure that this time is
used efficiently and effectively.

Intervene

What it is

Teams often experience behavioural problems which if not tackled can reduce effectiveness and lower morale. This tool gives a simple process for **intervening** and a range of levels at which it can be done.

The range of responses a leader can use when teams are going off track includes:

- **Do nothing (non-intervention)**

  Ignore it. Not important, or, doesn't affect team, or, team deals with it.

- **Off-line conversation (minimal intervention)**

  Talk to disruptive member outside meeting; give – and ask for – constructive feedback.

- **Impersonal group discussion (low intervention)**

  During meeting, raise team process concerns, revisit groundrules; critique and evaluate group behaviours; focus on how team encourages problem and what it can do to discourage it.

- **Off-line confrontation (medium intervention)**

  A more assertive version of the second point above. Use only when other attempts have failed. May lead to informal 'contract' between leader and member about changes to both.

- **In-group confrontation (high intervention)**

  Heavy. Leader challenges member in front of team. High risk, needs careful preparation, eg how to word the confrontation, what reactions to expect, how to avoid defensiveness and hostility. The purpose is to change behaviour, not punish the offender.

- **Expulsion from the group (don't do it)**

  You lose a lot as a team by kicking someone off it. So do they. Find another way. If all else fails, allow them not to attend meetings, but find other ways of bringing their input into the project.

How to use it

1. Be quite sure that you need to intervene – is it a real situation involving difficulty or disruption, and not just lighthearted fun!

2. Consciously select a level of intervention:

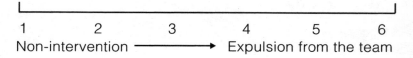

1   2   3   4   5   6
Non-intervention ⟶ Expulsion from the team

3. Check that you have observed and heard objectively – gather the facts.

4. Tell the team why you are intervening – use the facts (if done during team meeting).

5. Check with the team that they agree with your observations on the situation.

6. Ask the team for their ideas on how to resolve the situation,

   or/then

7. Suggest/agree with the team's ideas on resolution.

8. Back out – let them get on with it.

9. While ideally it should be the leader who intervenes, facilitators can do so either with the leader's prior permission or when the leader is clearly floundering and in need of help.

How it helps

The art of intervention is knowing when to do it. This tool will help you make a conscious choice on how and when to intervene when you see a team struggling rather than letting it slide.

 IF YOU'RE UNSURE, DON'T INTERVENE; LET THINGS DEVELOP FURTHER

Handle Poor Performance

What it is

Unfortunately there will be times when individual team members do not do what has been agreed. This tool outlines the options available to the team leader when this happens.

How to use it

1. Review the possible approaches

2. Identify the most appropriate way to tackle your problem

3. If it doesn't work, pick something more drastic!

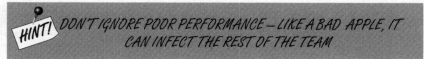

HINT! DON'T IGNORE POOR PERFORMANCE – LIKE A BAD APPLE, IT CAN INFECT THE REST OF THE TEAM

Checklist on handling poor performance:

Ways to approach individual performance problems:

✔ Speak privately with the person. Find out why.

✔ Clarify expectations with the person and, perhaps, with the whole team. Make sure all team members understand what is expected of them.

✔ Point out the impact of the behaviour. Make certain the person understands the consequences of a missed deadline or failure to complete a piece of work. Point out the impact on your customers/timetable/budget other team members, etc.

✔ Revisit team norms and groundrules. Remind the person that completing action items on time has been agreed to by all team members.

✔ Speak to the person's manager or close colleagues on the team. They may be able to provide some insight.

✔ Ask if the person needs help and, if so, what type. Help may be either additional hands to just get the work done or expert advice or training to improve skills.

✔ If the behaviour persists, you may have to ask the individual's manager to replace them on the team or start disciplinary action. Try to avoid this if possible, it can sour the whole team.

How it helps

Unless poor performance is tackled promptly it can have a demoralising effect on the rest of the team and reduce the chance of overall success. This tool identifies several ways of

5 Review performance

Team Leader Review

What it is

A complete review process for a team leader to use once work has begun to ensure that three sets of needs are met:

- The needs of the task
- The needs of the team
- The needs of the individuals (within the team).

How to use it

1. After the first few meetings, use the checklist to review your and your team's performance. You can either conduct the review privately or with a facilitator if you have one and you wish to have their contribution.

2. Consider each part in turn and make a list of action points for ones that need further work.

Task

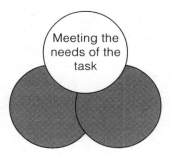

Task

✔ Purpose: Am I clear what the goal is?

✔ Responsibilities: Am I clear what mine are?

✔ Objectives: Have I agreed these with my sponsor and my manager?

✔ Plan: Have I worked one out to reach objectives

✔ Working conditions: Are these right for the job?

✔ Resources: Are these adequate (authority, materials)?

✔ Targets: Has each member clearly defined and agreed them?

✔ Authority: Is the line of authority clear? (Who am I accountable to?)

✔ Training: Are there any gaps in the specialist skills or abilities of individuals in the team required for the task?

✔ Priorities: Have I planned the time?

✔ Progress: Do I check this regularly and evaluate?

✔ Supervision: In case of my absence who covers for me?

Example: Do I set standards by my behaviour?

Team members

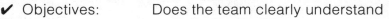

✔ Objectives: Does the team clearly understand and accept them?

✔ Standards: Do they know what standards of performance are expected?

✔ Size of team: Is the size correct?

✔ Team members: Are the right people working together? Is there a need for subgroups to be constituted?

✔ Team spirit: Do I look for opportunities for building teamwork into jobs? What activities should I arrange to develop team spirit?

✔ Groundrules: Are the rules seen to be reasonable? Am I fair and impartial in enforcing them?

✔ Conflict: Is conflict dealt with promptly? Do I take action on matters likely to disrupt the group?

✔ Consultation: Is this genuine? Do I encourage and welcome ideas and suggestions?

✔ Briefing: Is this regular? Does it cover current plans, progress and future developments?

✔ Represent: Am I prepared to represent the feelings of the group when required?

✔ Support: Do I visit people at their work when the team is apart? Do I then represent to the individual the whole team in my manner and encouragement?

Individual

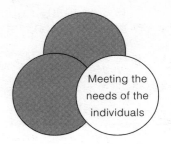

Meeting the needs of the individuals

✔ **Targets:** Have they been agreed and quantified?

✔ **Induction:** Does s/he really know the other team members and the organisation?

✔ **Achievement:** Does s/he know how his/her work contributes to the overall result?

✔ **Responsibilities:** Has s/he got a clear and accurate idea of what's expected? Can I delegate more to him/her?

✔ **Authority:** Does s/he have sufficient authority for his/her work?

✔ **Training:** Has adequate provision been made for training or retraining both technically and as a team member?

✔ **Recognition:** Do I emphasise people's successes? In failure, is criticism constructive?

✔ **Growth:** Does s/he see the chance of development?

✔ **Performance:** Is this regularly monitored?

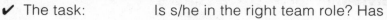

✔ The task:	Is s/he in the right team role? Has s/he the necessary resources?
✔ The person:	Do I know this person well? What makes him/her different from others?
✔ Time/attention:	Do I spend enough time with individuals listening, developing, counselling?
✔ Concerns:	Are these dealt with promptly?

How it helps

Reviewing is vital 'time out' for teams and their leaders. Completing reviews periodically permits the team leader to pinpoint barriers to effective performance and remove them.

This tool allows a team leader to review in detail his or her performance in order to ensure he/she take steps to meet the needs of the task, the team and the individual members.

Team Performance Review

What it is

This tool gives a review mechanism based on GRIPS which teams can use at any stage of their working life together.

How to use it

1. Issue the questionnaire that follows to all team members.

2. Ask individuals to complete the questionnaire privately.

3. Once everyone has completed it, ask group members to volunteer their scores for each part and encourage discussion.

4. Aim to reach consensus on each point and to allow each person the chance to air his/her views.

5. Note any action points separately, assigning each a person to be responsible and a deadline.

Team review questionnaire (GRIPS)

Goals

	Yes	?			No
Do we have a common understanding of our goal?	1	2	3	4	5
Are our objectives SMART?	1	2	3	4	5

Roles

Do we understand the role of our team in the organisation as a whole?	1	2	3	4	5
Do we understand and perform our roles within the team?	1	2	3	4	5
Do we make best use of our individual strengths?	1	2	3	4	5

Interactions

Do we regularly review how we communicate with each other?	1	2	3	4	5
Is everyone able to contribute fully?	1	2	3	4	5
Do we agree 'Groundrules' and use them?	1	2	3	4	5
Do we build on ideas and support each other?	1	2	3	4	5

Team processes

Do we have mutually acceptable ways of agreeing priorities, allocating time, handling conflict, making decisions, etc.?	1	2	3	4	5
Do we work on improving our processes?	1	2	3	4	5

Style

Does the style of the team leader enable effective teamwork?	1	2	3	4	5
Do we share leadership as necessary?	1	2	3	4	5

How it helps

This questionnaire enables a team to review its effectiveness and re-focus at any stage. It prevents resentment and team problems inhibiting the success of the team.

Team Behaviour and Individual Contributions Review

What it is

This tool focuses on the range of interpersonal behaviours that should be used and developed within a team over a period of time.

As well as looking at a team in terms of overall mechanics and/or behaviours, it can be helpful to review individual contributions in order to:

- generate personal feedback
- help personal development
- improve overall team performance.

How to use it

1. At the end of a team meeting, use the checklist to review the meeting.

2. Seek examples of each type of behaviours (it may be more effective to use an observer to collect this data during the meeting).

3. Identify the gaps or areas of poor performance.

4. Agree whether or not this needs to be tackled (and by whom).

5. Develop an action plan to improve the interpersonal behaviours in the team.

Team review checklist: task skills

Task skills	– actions aimed at getting the job done
The mechanics	Runs effective meetings – planned, agendas, minutes, evaluation of effectiveness, etc time frame for completion, use of tools and techniques, adequate room and equipment
Initiating	Clearly defines task objective, gets conversation going, keeps it going, stimulates ideas
Information gathering	Draws out relevant information, opinions, ideas, suggestions or concerns about the task
Information giving	Shares relevant information, opinions beliefs, etc (without prompting)
Clarifying and elaborating	Clears up confusion, gives examples, points out issues and other matters
Consensus testing	Pulls together whats been said, offers conclusions, etc (not just at the end but all the way through)
Summarising	Regularly summarises key points to ensure understanding and clarity and to move on debate

Team Behaviour/Contributions Review

Team review checklist: process skills

Maintenance or interpersonal skills	– actions aimed at keeping the team working together
Listening	Pays attention to the ideas and opinions of others, stay focused on others and doesn't interrupt
Participating	Keeps communication channels open. Helps others to participate, manages dominating speakers, encourages non-contributors, look for both verbal and behavioural participation
Encouraging	Friendly, warm, responsive, eye contact, non-judgemental
Compromising	Reduces tension, works out disagreement, admits error, looks for middle ground (even if it means yielding status)
Resolving conflict (harmonising)	Uses processes. Explores differences of opinion. Assesses the merits of the ideas assessed rather than the merits of who suggested them
Standard setting	Establishes group standards and takes steps to ensure they are maintained

How it helps

It is not sufficient for a team to exhibit the mechanics of effective meetings. It is also necessary to work on the personal behaviours outlined in this tool to communicate effectively.

Sharing personal feedback is also a useful step in building a close, interdependent team. This tool gives a constructive method for doing this.

6 Disband the team

Keep Others Informed

What it is

Effective teams ensure that others outside the team (customers, suppliers, line managers, colleagues, etc) are informed as appropriate of their progress/proposals/results, etc. This tool outlines some of the methods available and gives tips on how to use them.

How to use it

1. Written reports

Reports should be short, logical and lead to clear recommendations. The following format is suggested:

- Title page:
  - clear title
  - authors' names
  - date.
- Contents page.
- Introduction.
- Summary:
  - outline of results
  - summary of recommendations.
- Body of report:
  - clear, logical development of theme.
- Recommendations:
  - in full.
- Appendix:

DO

✔ Prepare:

- decide scope of report and target audience

✔ Collect material:

- distinguish between facts and opinions

✔ Arrange materials:

- sections/subsections
- headings/subheadings
- clear numbering system
- the steps of PDCA can be a useful framework

✔ Be brief:

- keep it simple

✔ Be clear:

- use diagrams and charts as much as possible

✔ Check for accuracy:

- facts, spelling, punctuation

✔ Sign the report

DON'T

✗ Be ambiguous

✗ Use long words and sentences

✗ Be repetitive

✗ Use jargon

✗ Include unnecessary information

2. Individual presentations

- Decide aim, topic, title.
- Decide at what level to present – this depends upon
  - audience roles
  - audience knowledge.
- Collect relevant data:
  - search widely
  - read around the subject.
- Prepare broad framework of presentation:
  - introduction
  - content headings
  - conclusions
  - recommendations.
- Select and arrange appropriate data.
- Write presentation – some people write it all out in detail, others just use paragraph headings.
- Plan visual aid requirements – keep them simple:
  - overheads?
  - slides?
  - video?
  - handouts?
- Read through presentation to check logic.
- Check presentation room and facilities.
- Rehearse:
  - preferably with constructive companion
  - decide where and when to ask for questions
  - check timing.
- Deliver:
  - address all of the audience
  - be interesting.
- Confirm conclusions and actions.
- Review afterwards – how could it have been better?

3. Group presentations

One powerful way to recognise the contribution of team members is to get **the team** to present its results as a group with each member having a part to play – even if it is only putting the visual aids onto the projector. This team effort is surprisingly effective in raising commitment and enthusiasm.

The same general rules apply as for individual presentations.

But to ensure maximum participation:

- Choose anchorperson.
- Share out the work:
  - preparation
  - presentation
  - visual aids
  - handouts
  - refreshments.
- Rehearse
- Check
  - timings
  - individual contributions
  - logic and continuity.
- Decide when to ask for questions
- Deliver:
  - acknowledge contributions to the project
  - emphasise achievements
  - include learning points.
- Review as a team.

Presentations generally

✔ Say what you are going to present

✔ Present it

✔ Then say what you have presented

✔ Confirm conclusions and actions

✔ Use examples, anecdotes and humour to keep it interesting

✔ Always use some form of visual aid

✔ Involve your audience wherever possible

4. Storyboards

A storyboard is a road map showing the progress of a team through the Quality Improvement Cycle. It is a very effective mechanism for sharing progress outside the team and encouraging feedback and ideas from others. Storyboards are often displayed beside traditional notice-boards, in corridors, canteens or even reception areas. *'Solve that problem'* Toolbox gives more details of the cycle and tools involved.

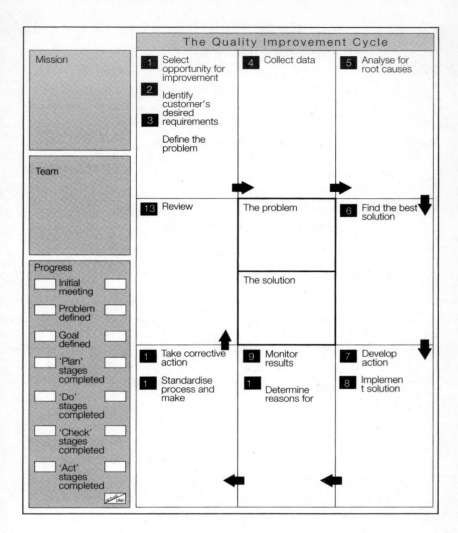

The Quality Improvement Cycle

Mission

Team

Progress

Initial meeting

Problem defined

Goal defined

'Plan' stages completed

'Do' stages completed

'Check' stages completed

'Act' stages completed

1. Select opportunity for improvement
2. Identify customer's desired requirements
3. Define the problem

4. Collect data

5. Analyse for root causes

13. Review

The problem

The solution

6. Find the best solution

1. Take corrective action
1. Standardise process and make

9. Monitor results
1. Determine reasons for

7. Develop action
8. Implement solution

How it helps

Effective communication with those outside the team can help to ensure success by avoiding the silence and assumptions which are the alternative. It also provides feedback to the team so avoiding wasted effort and resources.

Tie Up Loose Ends

What it is

When teams are going well and members enjoy being together, it is tempting to keep going beyond the useful life of the team. This tool gives guidelines on when and how to wind up a team and ensure that the loose ends are well tied.

How to use it

1. Decide if your team has 'finished':

   - have you achieved your objectives?
   - have your proposals been implemented?
   - is the new process stable and working as it should?
   - have you run out of useful things to do?
   - do your meetings feel less productive?
   - is the energy level starting to drop?

2. If you answer 'yes' to most of these then it is probably time to wind up, so:

   - propose this to the team and seek their agreement
   - do a full review of your results and performance
   - ensure your results are communicated to others along with your learning points
   - check there are measures in place to monitor ongoing performance and a process to pick up any slippage
   - decide if you need to meet periodically to review ongoing performance or whether this responsibility lies elsewhere
   - clean up your records and files to make it easy to reference them in the future. Get rid of useless material – it only clogs up space
   - decide how to recognise contributions that others have made to the team
   - plan a celebration!

How it helps

Teams which don't have a clean finish and leave loose ends and unfinished business are often less successful as their results will slip back quickly. This tool gives guidelines on how to avoid this happening and increase the chance of sustained success.

 DON'T LEAVE LOOSE ENDS, OTHERS MAY TRIP OVER THEM!

Recognise Success

What it is

The way in which people work is strongly influenced by the way leaders react. When working under pressure it is easy to only react negatively when there are problems or poor results. However, if you want people to try new ways to experiment or take risks in order to improve performance you must respond positively and constructively to their efforts as well as their results.

There are many ways in which recognition can be shown, both formal and informal.

This tool outlines a range of approaches to recognition for you to review and from which you can select.

How to use it

The following elements have all been incorporated successfully into formal recognition schemes by different companies:

- **Goals, measures, standards and targets**

  Unless performance is related back to the goals of the company/team/individual there is no objective way of assessing whether recognition is appropriate.

  Crosfield (a UK chemical company) formally assess every OFI (Opportunity for Improvement) against the contribution to company goals and provide a range of responses.

- **Training and development**

  While basic training to do a job should be provided for everyone, attendance and achievement in training can be a useful form of recognition (certificates and presentations).

Development through involvement in projects, visits, new tasks, deputising, etc is an ideal way of recognising earlier efforts.

Everyone who goes on any training course at Milliken receives a certificate signed by Roger Milliken.

- **OFIs**

  Putting forward suggestions for improvement should always be recognised in some way. Many companies have formalised this by giving tokens, gifts or even financial reward in recognition of the number of OFIs contributed or benefits achieved.

  At Paul Revere Inc (US financial services) employees receive bronze, silver or gold badges for contributing 10, 25 or 50 improvement ideas.

- **Publicity**

  Perhaps the most common form of recognition is publicising achievements through notice-boards, storyboards, newsletters, presentations and word of mouth. The level of publicity can be linked to the size of achievement.

  The Japanese tend to be quite formal with their recognition relying mostly on the presidential review process to highlight teams with good stories. Through the year the process builds up through departments, then units, then locations reviewing short presentations. Finally, the best teams are invited to a conference attended by the president and top executives.

- **Tokens**

  Tokens can be provided to be given spontaneously for specific acts (not just by managers). Badges, key rings, mugs are common.

  At Clarke American, every employee has a recognition 'cheque book' and can complete a 'cheque' and give it to anyone in the company. Accumulated cheques can be exchanged for small gifts. This not only encourages recognition but develops contacts and relationship across the business.

- **Awards/events**

Team/employee of the month/quarter/year are increasingly common. Clearly the criteria and method for assessment must be seen to be fair. Criteria can include customer employee feedback.

Milliken take any opportunity to put the 'fans in the stands'. As well as awards such as 'quality project of the period' and 'associate of the month' they have sharing rallies at which improvement teams, OFI proposers and exceptional performers take a bow.

- **Sharing benefits**

While recognition is not about financial reward there are times when companies choose to share a proportion of any financial benefit achieved with those involved or donate it to charity. This can, however, be decisive and criteria must be very clearly defined.

- **Planned visits**

Particularly where locations are split it is helpful for directors and managers to plan 'walking about'. Pre-briefing on OFIs, project teams, improvements achieved can make this a very powerful form of recognition. Do it often enough and it becomes the 'norm'.

Paul Revere has a PEET (Programme for Ensuring Everybody's Thanked) scheme which the Board uses to plan visits.

- ## Everyday behaviour

  Formal recognition will seem hollow and meaningless if not supported by day to day actions and behaviours. Informal, spontaneous recognition involves:

  - listening to ideas, suggestions, problems

  - encouraging and supporting involvement in improvement activities

  - being visible, accessible and approachable

  - having positive expectations about individual's ability and potential

  - understanding each individual's motivation needs and providing appropriate recognition for them

  - most of all giving praise and thanks for efforts, results and appropriate behaviour.

1. Review the various approaches to recognition. Which do you think would work for you?

2. Where will you start?

3. How will you go about it?

4. How will you ensure you are fair and consistent?

 RECOGNITION FEEDS FUTURE PERFORMANCE

Twenty ways to recognise

1. Send letters to improvement team members when they establish a team, thanking them for their involvement; send another one at the end of their project or key action, thanking them for their contribution.

2. Develop a 'behind the scenes' award specifically for those whose actions aren't usually in the limelight; make sure such awards are in the limelight.

3. Create a 'Best ideas of the year' booklet and include everyone's picture, name and description of their best ideas.

4. Feature a Quality team of the month and put their picture in a prominent place.

5. Honour peers who have helped you by recognising them at your (or their) staff meetings.

6. Let people attend meetings, committees, etc in your place when you're not available.

7. Involve teams with external customers and suppliers, sending them on appropriate visits to solve problems and look for opportunities.

8. Invite a team for coffee or lunch at any time, not necessarily when you need them for something.

9. Create a visibility wall to display information, posters, pictures, thanking individual employees and their teams, and describing their contributions.

10. When you are discussing an individual's or group's ideas with other people, peers, or higher management, make sure that you give them credit.

11. Mention someone's outstanding work or ideas during your own meetings and at meetings with your peers and management.

12. Take an interest in someone's development and set up appropriate training and experience to build on their initiatives.

13. Get your teams' pictures in the company newspaper.

14. Write a 'letter of praise' to people to recognise their specific contributions and accomplishments; send a copy to your boss.

15. Ask people to help you with a project you consider to be especially difficult but which provides real challenge.

16. Send a team to special seminars, workshops or meetings outside that cover topics they are especially interested in.

17. Ask your boss to send a letter of acknowledgement and thanks to individuals or groups that are making significant contributions.

18. Honour outstanding contributors with awards which are formally presented and publicised.

19. Have a stock of small gifts to give to people on the spot whom you 'catch doing things right'.

20. Promote, or nominate for promotion, those people who contribute most to improvement over a period of time.

How it helps

This tool identifies a range of approaches to recognition both formal and informal and suggests ways in which you can help to make it happen.

7 Improve work teams

Team Purpose Analysis

What it is

Team Purpose Analysis is a process which helps a team or unit:

- define its purpose and align with the business strategy and goals

- define the requirements, measurements and working relationships with its customers and suppliers

- identify its key processes and performance measures

- carry out an activity/task analysis to show what is currently being done and why

- identify whether or not each activity meets specific customer requirements and is right first time

- make immediate gains

- identify improvement projects for action.

In doing so, it introduces structure and priority to the improvement process so focusing and maintaining energy.

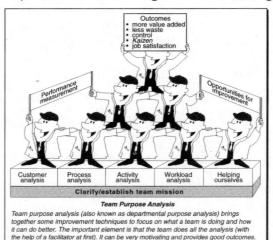

Team Purpose Analysis

Team purpose analysis (also known as departmental purpose analysis) brings together some improvement techniques to focus on what a team is doing and how it can do better. The important element is that the team does all the analysis (with the help of a facilitator at first). It can be very motivating and provides good outcomes.

How to use it

Over several months a team works through all or some of eight steps (depending on needs and priorities) addressing the following questions at each step:

1. Clarify/establish team mission

- What is the overall mission and what are the goals of the organisation?
- What is our contribution or role in achieving this mission?
- What are our overall responsibilities and main outputs?
- So what is our team mission?

2. Review customers and suppliers

- Who are our customers/suppliers?
- What are their/our requirements?
- What is our/their current performance?
- What measures/feedback mechanisms exist?
- How can outputs/inputs/measures be improved?

3. Review processes

- What are our key processes?
- Are they mapped?
- Are our performance measures adequate?
- How can our processes be improved?

4. Detailed activity analysis (on key processes to be improved)

- How long do they take?
- How much do they cost?
- Where is the waste?
- How often do things happen/go wrong?

- How well do we use our resources?
- Do effort and results seem in balance?
- What should we start/stop/do differently?

5. Workload management analysis

- What are our workload volumes?
- What are the daily/weekly/monthly/annual variations and trends?
- How well do we predict and/or manage variation?
- How well do we balance workload and resource?
- How can we improve our workload management?

6. Helping ourselves (internal processes)

- Are our individual roles/responsibilities sufficiently clear and coordinated?
- How well do we document our procedures and record our work?
- Do we meet our training needs sufficiently well?
- How well do we communicate with each other?
- How could we improve our teamworking?

7. Performance measures

Taking into account topics 1-6:

- What are our overall performance measures?
- Is sufficient, timely information available on these to take prompt action?

8. Opportunities for improvement

- What is the range of opportunities?
- What is urgent?
- How do we fix it?
- Can we make step by step improvements?
- What is in most need of a radical breakthrough improvement?

- Where do we need to use a project team?
- Do we need to benchmark ourselves?
- How shall we prioritise the bigger issues?
- Who is going to do what?
- How will we review our progress?

YOU DON'T HAVE TO COMPLETE 1-7 BEFORE DOING SOME OF 8!

How it helps

Team Purpose Analysis helps a team focus, prioritise and organise improvement activity. It helps to ensure that customer requirements are met, processes are managed, waste is removed and the team works effectively together. Unlike all of the other tools, which take minutes or hours, TPA is an ongoing process over many months.

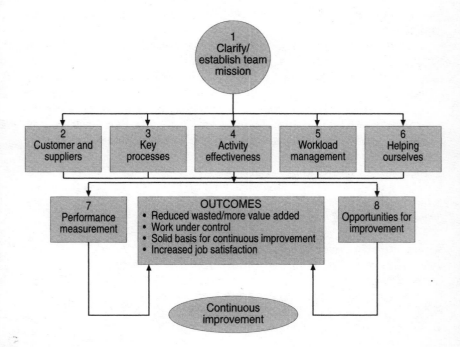

The Quest Toolbox Series

This series is different. It provides practical techniques, tested by experienced consultants with real organisations. Each tool follows a step-by-step approach, illustrated by worked examples. No theoretical explanations, just a wide choice of techniques to help stimulate, drive and manage change and the people that create it. Hundreds of directors, managers and team leaders worldwide are already using the series for personal reference, as handout material for training programmes or as an aid for project or improvement teams.

Steve Smith

Dr Smith has been helping organisations transform their performance and culture for 20 years. His unique experience of witnessing and consulting in global corporate change has helped him become regarded as one of the most progressive change management consultants of his generation.

A regular speaker and author, as well as conceptual thinker, Steve has facilitated the metamorphosis of over 150 organisations through the provision of timely, supportive and often pioneering consultancy advice.

A strong advocate of an holistic approach to business improvement, Steve works with his clients to define stretching, yet balanced strategies that work, and then helps to mobilise the whole organisation to turn those strategies into action.

Prior to forming Quest, Steve was a director of PA Consulting Services, where he worked for 11 years and founded the TQM division. A former lecturer at Aston University, Steve has also spent eight years with the Chrysler Corporation.

Acknowledgements
The Toolbox series has been drawn from the expertise of the entire Quest Worldwide consultancy team. Special thanks must go to Gillian Hayward for selecting and compiling tools for all five titles and to Mike Rayburn who developed and refined many of the techniques in *Make Things Happen!* Thanks also to Peter Holman, Tina Jacobs, Sue Hodder and the Quest support team.